DEPRESSION

Dr. Bimal Chhajer, MD

© **Author**

Published 2005
FUSION BOOKS
X-30, Okhla Industrial Area
Phase-2, New Delhi-110020
Phone-011-51611861-865
Fax-011-26386124,51611866
e-mail: sales@diamondpublication.com
www.diamondpublication.com

Cover & Book Design by
RITU SINHA
binsa_4@yahoo.com

ISBN- 81-89182-98-6
Price: Rs 50.00/US$ 2.95

Printed in India by
Best Photo Offset
New Delhi, India

Contents

Introduction

Depression is a "whole-body" illness, involving a person's body, mood, and thoughts. It affects the way one eats and sleeps, the way one feels about himself, and the way one thinks about things. A depressive disorder is not the same as a passing blue mood. It is not a sign of personal weakness or a condition that can be willed or wished away. People with a depressive illness cannot merely "pull themselves together" and get better. Without treatment, symptoms can last for weeks, months, or years. Appropriate treatment, however, can help most people who suffer from depression.

HOW DEPRESSION OCCURS?

Depression can occur due to a multitude of causes. It may be the result of a physical illness, bereavement, alcoholism, childbirth, or severe life events. It may occur as a result of problems that occurred in early childhood or as a result of the present difficulties relating to home or work.

WHY DEPRESSION OCCURS?

It has been suggested that people who tend to get depressed may have inherited a subtle chemical abnormality in their brain. This might make them more sensitive or susceptible to one or more of the life events mentioned above.

SYMPTOMS

Symptoms of depression may vary from person to person, and also depend on the severity of the problem. Depression causes changes in thinking, feelings, behaviour, and physical well-being.

Changes in thinking

People may experience problems with concentration and decision making. Some people report difficulty with short-term memory, forgetting things all the time. Negative thoughts and thinking are characteristic of depression. Pessimism, poor self-esteem, excessive guilt, and self-criticism are all common. Some people have self-destructive thoughts during a more serious depression.

Changes in Feelings

People may feel sad for no reason at all. Some people report that they no longer enjoy activities that they once found pleasurable. People might lack motivation, and become more apathetic. Some may feel "slowed down" and tired all the time. Sometimes irritability is a problem, and depressed person may have more difficulty controlling his temper. In the extreme, depression is characterized by feelings of helplessness and hopelessness.

Changes in Behaviour

Changes in behaviour during depression are reflective of the negative emotions being experienced. Patients might act more apathetic, because that's how they feel. Some people do not feel comfortable with other people, so social withdrawal is common. People may experience a dramatic change in appetite, either eating more or less. Because of the chronic sadness, excessive crying is common. Some people complain about everything, and act out their anger with temper outbursts. Sexual desire may disappear, resulting in lack of sexual activity. In the extreme, people may neglect their personal appearance, even neglecting basic hygiene. Needless to say, someone who is depressed does not do the optimum; so

V

work, productivity and household responsibilities suffer. Some people even have trouble getting out of bed.

Changes in Physical Well-being

We have already talked about the negative emotional feelings experienced during depression, but these are coupled with negative physical emotions as well. Chronic fatigue, despite spending more time sleeping, is common. Some people can't sleep, or don't sleep soundly. These individuals lay awake for hours, or awaken many times during the night, and stare at the ceiling. Others sleep many hours, even most of the day, although they still feel tired. Many people lose their appetite, feel slowed down by depression, and complain of many aches and pains. Others are restless, and can't sit still.

Now imagine these symptoms lasting for weeks or even months. Imagine feeling this way almost all the time. Depression is present if you experience many of these symptoms for at least several weeks. Of course, it's not a good idea to diagnose yourself. If you think that you might be depressed, see a psychologist as soon as possible. A psychologist can assess whether you are depressed, or just under a lot of stress and feeling sad. Remember, depression is treatable. Instead of worrying about whether you are depressed, do something about it, even if you don't feel like it right now.

Depressive disorders come in different forms. There are several different diagnoses for depression, mostly determined by the intensity of the symptoms, the duration of the symptoms, and the specific cause of the symptoms, if that is known.

1. TYPES OF DEPRESSIVE DISORDERS

Psychology provides information on the following depressive disorders.

1. Major Depression

Major depression is characterized by a combination of symptoms, including sad mood (see symptom list), that interfere with the ability to work, sleep, eat, and enjoy once-pleasurable activities. Disabling episodes of depression can occur once, twice, or several times in a lifetime. It continues more then two weeks.

2. Dysthymic Disorder

This refers to a low to moderate level of depression that persists for at least two years, and often longer. While the symptoms are not as severe as a major depression, they are more enduring and resistant to treatment. Some people with dysthymia develop a major depression sometime during the course of their depression.

3. Unspecified Depression

This category is used to help researchers who are studying other specific types of depression, and do not want their data confounded with marginal diagnoses. It includes people with a serious depression, but not quite severe enough to have a diagnosis of a major depression. It also includes people with chronic, moderate depression, which has not been present long enough for a diagnosis of a dysthymic disorder. (You get the idea!)

4. Adjustment Disorder, with Depression

This category describes depression that occurs in response to a major life stressor or crisis.

5. Bipolar Depression (Mania)

This type includes both high and low mood swings, as well as a variety of other significant symptoms not present in other depressions.

6. SAD (Seasonal Affective Disorder)

This occurs due to lack of light. People in cold countries usually get this syndrome due to lack of sun rays in winter.

2. THE SYMPTOMS OF DEPRESSION

One should talk to a psychologist for an evaluation, if one experiences several of the following symptom clusters, and the symptoms persist for more than two weeks, or if they interfere with one work or one's family life. However, not everyone with depression experiences all of these symptoms, and the severity of the symptoms also varies from person to person.

When a person should consult a doctor

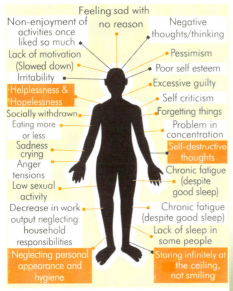

Feeling sad with no reason

Non-enjoyment of activities once liked so much

Negative thoughts/thinking

Lack of motivation (Slowed down)

Pessimism

Irritability

Poor self esteem

Helplessness & Hopelessness

Excessive guilty

Self criticism

Socially withdrawn

Forgetting things

Eating more or less

Problem in concentration

Sadness crying

Self-destructive thoughts

Anger tensions

Chronic fatigue (despite good sleep)

Low sexual activity

Chronic fatigue (despite good sleep)

Decrease in work output neglecting household responsibilities

Lack of sleep in some people

Neglecting personal appearance and hygiene

Staring infinitely at the ceiling, not smiling

* If these symtoms continue for more than one week then one should consult Psycotherapist.

* If one has the symptoms highlighted in the box than hospitalization is required.

DEPRESSION

* Persistent sad, anxious, or "empty" mood
* Loss of interest or pleasure in your usual activities, including sex
* Restlessness, irritability, or excessive crying
* Feelings of guilt, worthlessness, helplessness, hopelessness, pessimism
* Sleeping too much or too little, early morning awakening
* Appetite and/or weight loss or overeating and weight gain
* Decreased energy, fatigue, feeling "slowed down"
* Thoughts of death or suicide, or suicide attempts
* Difficulty in concentrating, remembering, or making decisions
* Persistent physical symptoms that do not respond to treatment, such as headaches, digestive disorders, or chronic pain

9

HOW THE BRAIN WORKS

ANATOMY OF BRAIN

The human brain is the most extraordinary organ in the body. It controls our immensely completed body function, acting as the ringmaster for all the other systems in the body, including both the unconscious mechanisms such as our heartbeat, breathing and digestion, and the conscious mechanisms such as speech and movement. The brain function starts with the billions of nerve cells, or neurons, which create a mesh of electrical impulses which acts like a huge circuit board, stimulating the various thought, motor and sensory pathways in the body, thus allowing us to do the simplest thing, such as scratching our head or whistling a tune, or the most complex, such as composing a symphony or discovering the theory of relativity, a range of sophisticated mechanisms that are not available to other mammals. If there is a breakdown at any point in this complex electrical circuitry, then the activity in the brain is reduced. The area of brain implicated in depression are forebrain and limbic system. They work as follows:

FOREBRAIN (Frontal Cortex)

The frontal cortex in the brain if overstimulated may give manic depressives. The different areas in the frontal cortex interact with each other via the neural pathways, and if one area is damaged and malfunctioning the others will also be affected—like memory, concentration, consciousness of self and emotional pain.

LIMBIC SYSTEM Grey Matter (Cerebral Cortex)

Cerebral cortex crammed with neurons and their little helpers, the glial cells, is crumpled up into folds so that it covers the other brain structures and fits neatly inside the human head.

Neurons: Neurons are the nerve cells in the brain, around 100 billion in number. Neuron helps to send or receive messages from other neurons in the brain in a complex electrical interaction for the purpose of stimulating activity in the numerous systems around the body. Neurons stimulate vision, recognition, the decision to speak, the words you choose, your hand reaching out to touch them, the sensation of that touch, the ability to process how your friend is reacting and your pleasure in the encounter.

Glial Cells: Glial cells, around 1000 billion in number, are responsible for supporting neurons by feeding them vital nutrients and providing the best biochemical environment for the nerve cells in brain.

Neurotransmitters: Neurons are not actually connected to one another. So to help the electrical brain messages over the tiny gap, called a synapse, between one neuron and the next there are chemical molecules, called neurotransmitters, released from the neurons to bridge the gap. These include serotonin, noradrenaline and dopamine and low levels of these particular culprits seem to be involved in depressive illness.

Besides this there are many specific brain structures that are strongly associated with the symptoms of depressive illness, but it is important to remember that no one structure works alone. They are:

Hypothalamus: An area of the brain releases hormones which in turn trigger the

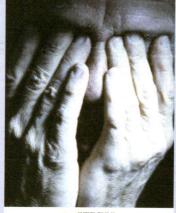

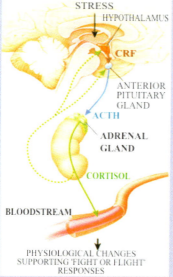

STRESS

HYPOTHALAMUS

CRF

ANTERIOR
PITUITARY
GLAND

ACTH

**ADRENAL
GLAND**

CORTISOL

BLOODSTREAM

PHYSIOLOGICAL CHANGES
SUPPORTING 'FIGHT OR FLIGHT'
RESPONSES

pituitary gland to release more hormones, which in turn affect various glands in the body. These glands, including the thyroid and adrenal glands, then produce hormones, such as adrenaline (epinephrine), noradrenaline (norepinephrine) and cortisol which affect our mood. Depression occurs when, the levels of cortisol and stress hormone adrenaline become too high.

Pineal Gland: The pineal gland secretes the hormone melatonin, which helps us sleep. If this hormone is not being produced in the right amount, then our body rhythms become disturbed, our sleep patterns go haywire. High levels of melatonin in the body are linked with seasonal affective disorder (SAD)

Amygdala: The amygdala, a small walnut-shaped organ in the brain, plays a powerful role in emotional responses, such as fear and negative emotions. If this organ is damaged, then the person will not be able to respond adequately to normal emotional stimuli, which can make them anxious, and can trigger the stress hormones.

4. WHAT HAPPENS IN THE BRAIN DURING DEPRESSION

The areas of the brain which get affected during depression are the forebrain and the limbic system.

Many structures of the forebrain appear to be involved in depression, although it is not certain if a disturbance to these brain areas causes depression, or if they are simply affected in the course of the disease. The brain areas involved include the frontal and temporal lobes of the forebrain, the basal nuclei and parts of the limbic system including the hippocampus, amygdala and the cingulate gyrus. The cerebral cortex controls thinking and it is likely that abnormalities in this part of the forebrain are responsible for the negative thoughts that are typical of depression.

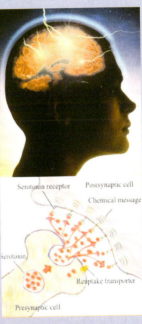

The hypothalamus and the pituitary gland may also play a role in depression, as they are involved in hormonal control and increased levels of some hormones may play a role in maintaining a depressed state.

If the body is placed under stress the hypothalamus-pituitary-adrenal axis becomes activated. The hypothalamus produces corticotropin releasing factor (CRF) which is hypothesised to play a role in the precipitation of certain forms of depression. CRF

13

SEROTONIN Lets you sleep   NORADRENALIN Gives you energy   DOPAMINE Sets your pleasure and pain levels

stimulates the pituitary gland to secrete adrenocorticotropic hormone, which in turn stimulates the adrenal glands to release cortisol. Cortisol depresses mood and approximately 50% of people with severe depression have high cortisol levels.

In the brainstem the raphe nuclei and the locus coeruleus are involved in the transmission of signals to other parts of the brain, and are likely to be involved in depression. An imbalance or deficiency of the neurotransmitters, serotonin, noradrenaline and dopamine are implicated in depression, although it may be a change in receptor function and not neurotransmitter concentration that causes depression.

C a u s e s   o f   d e p r e s s i o n

PREDISPOSING FACTORS
* *Family tendency*
* *Insecurity*
* *Dependancy*

PRECIPITATING EVENTS
* *Death of relative, close friend*
* *Loss in business, loss of job*

* *Long-term illness*
* *Addiction*
* *Divorce*
* *Retirement*
* *Loss of income*

MAINTAINING FACTORS
* *Unhappy marriage*

* *Separation from family*
* *Chronic shortage of money*
* *Trouble in office*
* *Court cases pending*
* *Quarrel at home*
* *Excessive debt*
* *Lack of family support*

5. PEOPLE AT THE HIGHER RISK

WOMEN AT GREATER RISK FOR DEPRESSION THAN MEN

Major depression and dysthymia affect twice as many women as men. This two-to-one ratio exists regardless of racial and ethnic background or economic status. The same ratio has been reported in eleven other countries all over the world. Men and women have about the same rate of bipolar disorder (manic depression), though its course in women typically has more depressive and fewer manic episodes. Also, a greater number of women have the rapid cycling form of bipolar disorder, which may be more resistant to standard treatments.

Many factors unique to women are suspected to play a role in developing depression. Research is focused on understanding these factors, including reproductive, hormonal, genetic or other biological factors; abuse and oppression; interpersonal factors; and certain psychological and personality characteristics. But, the specific causes of depression in women remain unclear. Many women exposed to these stress factors do not develop depression. Remember, depression is a treatable psychological problem, and treatment is effective for most women.

OLDER PEOPLE AT RISK

Old people are particularly vulnerable to depression. Research shows that one out of every twelve persons aged sixty-five or over is suffering from major depression, although it seems the symptoms often go unrecognized. You might think it reasonable that old people, particularly if they are lonely, ill or in care, might suffer from an increased incidence of depression. Much of this increase may be explained by the prevalence of disease in the elderly that are associated with depression, such as dementia, stroke and parkinson's. Also, old people are twice as likely to be on medication, some of which is linked to symptoms of depressive illness, such as some beta-blockers used to lower blood pressure.

SOCIAL DEPRIVATION

Social deprivation has long been thought to be a precipitating factor in depressive illness. If you live with the stress of unemployment or low-paid work where you are not properly valued, the humiliation of benefits, and the worry about whether you will have enough

money to pay the bills and feed the children, it is hardly surprising that you might be more prone to depressive symptoms. Research shows that people suffering socioeconomic deprivation have a higher rate of depression as it naturally inclines a person to drift into poverty, as they can no longer hold down a job or relationship.

A recent study at Cornell University in America found that inadequate food intake or a poor diet leads to depression.

RICH PEOPLE GET DEPRESSED TOO

Depression can strike anyone even celebrities, eminent scientists, politicians, writers, artists and people who have to the casual observer, the most perfect lives.

6. DEPRESSION AND HEART DISEASE

Depression can strike anyone. However, research over the past two decades has shown that people with heart disease are more likely to suffer from depression than otherwise healthy people, and conversely, that people with depression are at greater risk of developing heart disease. Furthermore, people with heart disease who are depressed have an increased risk of death after a heart attack compared to those who are not depressed. Depression may make it harder to take the medications needed and to carry out the treatment for heart disease. Treatment for depression helps people manage both diseases, thus enhancing survival and quality of life. Risk factors for heart disease other than depression include high levels of cholesterol (a fat-like substance) in the blood, high blood

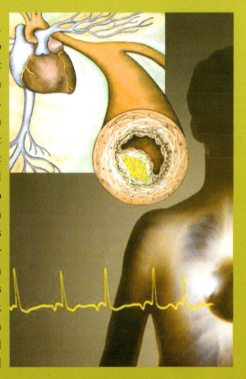

pressure, and smoking. On the average, each of these doubles the chance of developing heart disease. Obesity and physical inactivity are other factors that can lead to heart disease. Regular exercise, good nutrition, and smoking cessation are key to controlling the risk factors for heart disease.

Depression and anxiety disorders may affect heart rhythms and alter blood clotting. Depression also appears to be important as a risk factor for high blood pressure, they are found to double or triple the risk of developing high blood pressure. They can also lead to elevated insulin and cholesterol levels. These risk factors, with obesity, form a group of signs and symptoms that often serve as both a predictor of and a response to heart disease. Furthermore, depression or anxiety may result in chronically elevated levels of stress hormones, such as cortisol and adrenaline. As high levels of stress hormones are signalling a "fight or flight" reaction, the body's metabolism is diverted away from the type of tissue repair needed in heart disease.

Despite the enormous advances in brain research in the past 20 years, depression often goes undiagnosed and untreated. Persons with heart disease, their families and friends, and even their physicians and cardiologists (physicians specializing in heart disease treatment) may misinterpret depression's warning signs, mistaking them for inevitable accompaniments to heart disease. Symptoms of depression may overlap with those of heart disease and other physical illnesses. However, skilled health professionals will recognize the symptoms of depression and inquire about their duration and severity, diagnose the disorder, and suggest appropriate treatment.

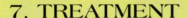

7. TREATMENT

The most commonly used treatments for depression are psychotherapy and antidepressant medication, or a combination of the two. Which of these is the right treatment for an individual depends on the nature and severity of the depression and, to some extent, on individual preference. In mild or moderate depression, psychotherapy is perhaps the most appropriate treatment. But in severe or incapacitating depression, medication is generally recommended, in addition to psychotherapy. In combined treatment, medication can relieve physical symptoms quickly, while psychotherapy allows you to learn more effective ways of handling your problems.

MEDICINES

The first generation drugs used for treating depression are:

1. *TCA (Inhibit Reuptake of Monoamines):*
Most common names of TCA used to treat depression are Tryptomer, Sarotena, Eliwel, Depnil, Doxydep.

2. *MAOI (Monoamine Oxidase Inhibitors):* These drugs block the activity of the enzyme responsible for breaking down neurotransmitters noradrenaline and serotonin. These drugs are the oldest antidepressant drugs, and are not used very often these days because of their unpleasant side effects. Example: Phenelzine (Nardil), Isocarboxazid(Marplan), Tranylcypromine (Parnate).

Second generation drugs used for treating depression are:

1. *SNRI (Selective Noradrenaline and serotonin Re-uptake inhibitor):* SNRI helps to raise the level of nonadrenaline as well as serotonin. Example: Venlafaxin (Venlor, Ven, Venlift).

2. *SSRI (Selective serotonin re-uptake inhibitor):* These are a new generation anti

depression drugs and are most commonly used to treat depression with least side effects. These drugs increase the level of neurotransmitter serotonin in the brain by preventing the existing serotonin from being reabsorbed into the cells. Example: Fluoxetine (Prodac), Paroxetine (Xet), Sertraline (Resert), Citalopram (Citola, Topdep), Fluvoxamine (Fluvoxin).

3. *NARI (Selective Noradrenaline Re-uptake Inhibitor):* This drug raises the levels of the neurotransmitter noradrenaline in the brain by blocking the reabsorption of existing noradrenaline. This drug is used as an alternative to SSRIs and SNRIs. Example: Reboxetine (Edronax).

4. *NaSSA (Noradrenergic and Specific Serotonergic Antidepressant):* This drug helps in improving the transmission of noradrenaline and serotonin between the neurons. This is one of newer antidepressants recently introduced on to the market. Example: Mirtazapine (Zispin, Nassa, Mirt).

5. *Nefazodone:* This is another new antidepressant drug which helps to increase the level of noradrenaline in the brain. Example: Nefazodone (Dutonin, Serzone).

6. *Trazodone:* This drug is not related to other currently prescribed antidepressants, either in terms of its molecular structure or pharmacologically. It increases the availability of serotonin. Example: Trazodoen (Tazodac, Trazonil, Traze)

7. *Tricyclic Antidepressants:* These raise levels of noradrenaline and serotonin in the brain by inhibiting the reabsorption of neurotransmitters noradrenaline and serotonin. These drugs are less often used in treating depression these days because of their raft of unpleasant side effects and the fact that an overdose can prove fatal. Example: Amitriptyline (Amit, Latilin, ryptomer, Sarotena), Clomipramine

(Anafranil, Clomidac, Depnil, Clinil), Imipramine (Depsol, Depranil, Depsin) Nortriptyline (Nordep, Nortin, Primox), Amoxapine (Demolax), Dexepin (Doxeped, Doxin), Trimipramine (Surmontil).

8. Tetracyclic antidepressants: They raise the levels of serotonin and noradrenaline in the brain. These act in is the same way as tricyclic antidepressants. Example: Mianserin (non-proprietary). Maprotiline (Ludiomil), Lofepramine (Gamanil).

ALTERNATIVE THERAPY

Alternative therapy to treat depression are:

1. Excessive light treatment.
2. Support interpersonal relationship (Support from family and friends)
3. No holding of emotions
4. Health-coping skills
5. *Yogasana*
6. *Pranayama (Kapal Bhati, Ujjayi)*
7. *Kayotsarga*

8. Positive meditation
9. Psychotherapy
a) Supportive counselling
b) Cognitive therapy
c) Interpersonal therapy
d) Behavioural therapy

PSYCHOTHERAPY

Psychotherapy is used to treat depression in several ways. Firstly, supportive counselling can help to ease the pain of depression, and can address the hopelessness of depression. Secondly, cognitive therapy works to change the pessimistic ideas, unrealistic expectations, and overly critical self-evaluations that create the depression and sustain it. Cognitive therapy can help the depressed person recognize which life problems are critical, and which are minor. It also helps them to develop positive life goals, and a more positive self-assessment. Thirdly, problem-solving therapy is usually needed to change the areas of the person's life that are creating significant stress, and contributing to the depression. This may require behavioural therapy to develop better coping skills, or interpersonal therapy, to assist in resolving relationship problems. Research has shown that these psychotherapies are particularly helpful for treating depression.

8. HEALING DEPRESSION WITH YOGA

In the Yoga Sutras, Patanjali states that our inner obstacles create mental distraction, which in turn leads to Daurmanasya, depression. These inner obstacles can be removed by the practice of *yogic* techniques asana, meditation and pranayama.

Yoga is contraindicated with severe depression or other serious mental disorders. Severe or chronic depression (over four weeks) needs to be treated by a medical professional. *Yoga* should be used to supplement conventional therapy, not replace it.

***Yoga* postures:** *Yoga* postures will activate and move prana in the body, open the heart center, stimulate and nervous system and balance the body-mind-spirit.

***Pranayama*:** *Yogic* breathing exercises can calm the mind, reduce stress and alleviate anxiety.

***Yogic* Meditation:** Meditation reduces stress, calms the mind, reduces negativity and creates a positive mental attitude.

Yoga's regulating and energizing properties can help alleviate many of the symptoms of mild depression. *Yoga* postures will activate and move prana in the body, open the heart center, stimulate the nervous system and balance the body-mind-spirit. If you are mostly feeling frustration, use postures that open the insides of the legs (boundangle *baddhakonasana*), standing angle—*dandayamana-konasana,* half circle—ardhchakra-sana, half moon—*ardhchandrasana*). For feelings of sadness and grief, focus on postures that open the chest and inner arms (fish—matsyasana, boat—*navasana*). For low motivation or low energy use back and forward

23

bending postures (cobra—*bhujangasana*, sun—*suryanamaskar*). A slow, gentle practice is recommended; do not overexert yourself or you may end up more tired than you began. Practising *Yoga* as often as possible; on a daily is most beneficial.

Other *yogic* exercises are very effective at moving through depression. Practise *Kapalabhati Pranayama* to energize the body and *Nadi Sodhana Pranayama* to reduce stress and anxiety. Meditation reduces stress, calms the mind, reduces negativity and creates a positive attitude. Severe or chronic depression (over four weeks) needs to be treated by a medical professional. If you are having thoughts of suicide, get help immediately.

Yoga is contraindicated with severe depression or other serious mental disorders. A *yoga* practice should be used to supplement conventional therapy, not replace it.

Asana is defined as "posture;" its literal meaning is "seat." Originally, the *asanas* served as stable postures for prolonged meditation. More than just stretching, *asanas* open the energy channels, *chakras* and psychic centers of the body. *Asanas* purify and strengthen the body and control and focus the mind. *Asana* is one of the eight limbs of classical *Yoga*, which states that *asana* should be steady and comfortable, firm yet relaxed.

When holding a *yoga* posture, make sure you can breathe slowly and deeply,

Yoga is a relaxing form of exercise that can help alleviate depression. Meditation and *yoga* poses can help you attack the root cause of depression—the feeling that you can't handle the demands of your life. It tones the nervous system, stimulates circulation, promotes concentration, and energizes your mind and body.

BREATHING *(PRANAYAMA)*

The breathing exercise known as *Ujjayi Pranayama* is beneficial for healing depression.

YOGA ASANAS RECOMMENDED FOR DEPRESSION

1. The sun salutation (12 repetitions a day) 1. Bow pose *(Dhanurasana)*
3. Corpse pose *(Shavasana)* 4. *Maha Mudra*
5. Plow pose *(Halasana)*, 6. Shoulder stand *(Sarvangasana)*
7. *Vajrasana* (Sitting on the heels)

RELAXATION EXERCISE *(KAYOTSARGA)* FOR DEPRESSION

Try the following tense-relax exercise as you lie in the corpse pose:

1. As you inhale through your nose, tighten the muscles in your knees, calves, ankles, feet, and toes. Hold the tension, then relax and exhale.
2. Inhale, tensing all of these parts as well as your abdomen, pelvis, hips, and thighs. Hold them taut, then relax and exhale.
3. Tense the muscles in your neck, shoulders, arms, elbows, waist, hands, fingers, chest as well as muscles in your trunk and legs. Hold the tension, then relax and exhale.
4. Finally, starting with your scalp, face, and head, tense all of your body muscles. Hold the tension, then relax and exhale. Feel how all of the tension has melted away from your body

9. ADOLESCENT DEPRESSION

Definition: A disorder occurring during the teenage years marked by persistent sadness, discouragement, loss of self-worth, and loss of interest in usual activities.

CAUSES AND RISKS

Depression can be a transient response to many situations and stresses. In teenage, depressed mood is common because of the normal maturation process, the stress associated with it, the influence of sex hormones and independence conflicts with parents.

It may also be a reaction to a disturbing event, such as the death of a friend or relative, a breakup with a boyfriend or girlfriend, or failure at school. Teenagers who have low self-esteem, are highly self-critical and who feel little sense of control over negative events are particularly at risk to become depressed when they experience stressful events.

True depression in teens is often difficult to diagnose because of normal adolescent behavior is marked by mood swing, with alternating periods of feeling 'the world is a great place' and 'life sucks'. These moods may alternate over a period of hours or days.

Persistent depressed mood, faltering school performance, failing relations with family and friends, substance abuse, and other negative behaviors may indicate a serious depressive episode. These symptoms may be easy to recognize, but depression in adolescents often manifests very differently than these classic symptoms.

Excessive sleeping, change in eating habits, even criminal behavior (like shop lifting) may be signs of depression. Another common symptom of adolescent depression is an obsession with death, which may take the form either of suicidal thoughts or of fears about death and dying.

Long-term depressive illness usually has its onset in the teen or young adult years -- about 15% to 20% of teens have experienced a serious episode of depression, which is similar to the proportion of adults suffering from depression.

Adolescent girls are twice as likely as boys to experience depression. Risk factors include stressful life events, particularly loss of a parent to death or divorce; child abuse; unstable care giving, poor social skills; chronic illness; and family history of depression.

PREVENTION

Periods of depressed mood are common in most adolescents. However, supportive interpersonal relationships and healthy coping skills can help prevent such periods from leading to more severe depressive symptoms. Open communication with your teen can help identify depression earlier.

Counselling may help teens deal with periods of low mood. Cognitive behavioral therapy, which teaches depressed people ways of fighting negative thoughts and recognizing them as symptoms, not the truth about their world, is the most effective non-medication treatment for depression. Ensure that counselors or psychologists sought are trained in this method.

For adolescents with a strong family history of depression, or with multiple risk factors, episodes of depression may not be preventable. For these teens, early identification and prompt and comprehensive treatment of depression may prevent or postpone further episodes.

SYMPTOMS

* Depressed or irritable mood
* Temper, agitation
* Loss of interest in activities, apathy
* Reduced pleasure in daily activities
* Inability to enjoy activities which used to be sources of pleasure
* Change in appetite, usually a loss of appetite but sometimes an increase
* Change in weight (unintentional weight loss or unintentional weight gain)
* Persistent difficulty falling asleep or staying asleep (insomnia)
* Excessive daytime sleepiness
* Fatigue
* Difficulty concentrating
* Difficulty making decisions
* Memory loss (amnesia) episodes
* Preoccupation with self
* Feelings of worthlessness, sadness, or self-hatred
* Excessive or inappropriate feelings of guilt
* Acting-out behaviour (missing curfews, unusual defiance)
* Thoughts about suicide or obsessive fears or worries about death
* Plans to commit suicide or actual suicide attempt
* Excessively irresponsible behaviour pattern

If these symptoms persist for at least two weeks and cause significant distress or difficulty functioning, treatment should be sought.

SIGNS AND TESTS

* Physical examination and blood tests to rule out medical causes for the symptoms (for example: hypothyroidism, pregnancy, kidney disease).

* Evaluation for substance abuse -- heavy drinking, frequent marijuana smoking, and other drug use can be both causes and consequences of depression. Past practice in

addiction treatment was to assume depression was only a symptom of use, not a potential cause, and it was left untreated. Research now shows that this leads to increased risk of relapse. If a substance abuse problem is found, be sure that psychiatric evaluation doesn´t stop at diagnosing this, but continues to assess depression and other potential psychiatric problems.

* Psychiatric evaluation to assess a history of persistent sad, empty, or irritable mood and loss of interest or pleasure in normal activities. Evaluation for other potentially co-existing psychiatric disorders (such as anxiety, mania, or schizophrenia).

* Assessment of suicidal/homicidal risks.

* Information from family members or school personnel is often helpful in identifying depression in teens.

TREATMENT

Treatment options for adolescents with depression are similar to those for depressed adults, and include psychotherapy and antidepressant medications. However, one major antidepressant drug, Paxil, now has a warning "NOT to be given to children under 18".

Family therapy may be helpful if family conflict is contributing to depression. Support from family or teachers to help with school-related problems may also be needed. Occasionally, hospitalization in a psychiatric unit may be required for individuals with severe depression, or if they are at risk of suicide.

Because of the behavior problems that often co-exist with adolescent depression, many parents are tempted to utilize punitive solutions like "boot camps", "wilderness programs", or "emotional growth schools."

These programs frequently utilize non-professional staff and use confrontational therapies and harsh punishments. There is no scientific evidence, which supports use of these programs. In fact, there is a growing body of research, which suggests that they can actually harm teens, particularly sensitive teens with depression.

Depressed teens who act out may also become involved with the criminal justice system. Parents are often advised not to intervene, but to "let them experience consequences." Unfortunately, this can also harm teens through exposure to more deviant peers and reduction in educational opportunities. A better solution is to get the best possible legal advice and search for treatment on your own, which gives parents more control over techniques used and options.

Though a large percentage of teens in the criminal justice system have mental disorders like depression, few juvenile prisons, "boot camps" or other "alternative to prison" programs provide adequate treatment.

COMPLICATIONS

Teenage suicide is associated with depression as well as many other factors. Depression frequently interferes with school performance and interpersonal relationships. Teens with depression often have other psychiatric problems, such as anxiety disorders.

Depression is also commonly associated with violence and reckless behavior. Drug, alcohol, and tobacco abuse frequently coexist with depression. Adolescents with additional psychiatric problems usually require longer and more intensive treatment.

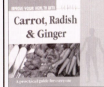

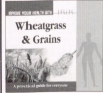

Health Books

M. Subramaniam

Unveiling the Secrets of Reiki 195.00
Brilliant Light (Reiki Grand Master Manual) 195.00
At the Feet of the Master (Manal Reiki) 195.00

Sukhdeepak Malvai

Natural Healing with Reiki 100.00

Pt. Rajnikant Upadhyay

Reiki (For Healthy, Happy & Comfortable Life)...................95.00
Mudra Vigyan (For Health & Happiness)............................60.00

Sankalpo

Neo Reiki 150.00

Dr. Shiv Kumar

Aroma Therapy...95.00
Causes, Cure & Prevention of Nervous Diseases..............75.00
Diseases of Digestive System 75.00
Asthma-Allergies (Causes & Cure)....................................75.00
Eye-Care Without Glassess *(Including Better Eye Sight)* 75.00
Stress *(How to relieve from Stress, A Psychlogical Study)*.............75.00

Dr. Satish Goel

Causes & Cure of Blood Pressure 75.00
Causes & Cure of Diabetes..60.00
Causes & Cure of Heart Ailments.....................................75.00
Pregnancy & Child Care 95.00
Ladies' Slimming Course 95.00
Acupuncture Guide 50.00
Acupressure Guide 50.00
Acupuncture & Acupressure Guide 95.00
Walking for Better Health 95.00
Nature Cure for Health & Happiness.................................95.00
A Beacon of Hope for the Childless Couples 60.00
Sex for All 75.00

Dr. Kanta Gupta

Be Your Own Doctor *(a books about herbs & their use)* 60.00

Dr. M.K. Gupta

Causes, Cure & Prevention of High Blood Cholesterol 60.00

Dr. B.R. Kishore

Vatsyayan's Kamasutra 95.00
The Manual of Sex & Tantra 95.00

Acharya Bhagwan Dev

Yoga for Better Health 95.00
Pranayam, Kundalini aur Hathyoga...................................95.00

Dr. S.K. Sharma

Add Inches 60.00
Shed Weight Add Life 60.00
Alternate Therapies 95.00
Miracles of Urine Therapy 60.00
Meditation & Dhyan Yoga *(for Spiritual Discipline)* 95.00
A Complete Guide to Homeopathic Remedies................120.00
A Complete Guide to Biochemic Remedies 60.00
Common Diseases of Urinary System...............................95.00
Allopathic Guide for Common Disorders 125.00
E.N.T. & Dental Guide 95.00
Wonders of Magnetotherapy 95.00
Family Homeopathic Guide 95.00
Health in Your Hands 95.00
Food for Good Health..95.00
Juice Therapy 75.00
Tips on Sex..75.00

Dr. Renu Gupta

Hair Care *(Prevention of Dandruff & Baldness)*..........................75.00
Skin Care 75.00
Complete Beautician Course *(Start a Beauty Parlour at Home)* 95.00
Common Diseases of Women 95.00

Dr. Rajiv Sharma

First Aid 95.00
Causes, Cure and Prevention of Children's Diseases........75.00

Dr. Nishtha

Diseases of Respiratory Tract *(Nose, Throat, Chest & Lungs)*..95.00
Backache *(Spondylitis, Cervical, Arthrtis Rheumatism)* 95.00
Ladies' Health Guide *(With Make-up Guide)* 95.00

Books can be requisitioned by V.P.P. Postage charges will be Rs. 20/- per book. For orders of three books the postage will be free.

 **DIAMOND BOOKS**

X-30, Okhla Industrial Area, Phase-II, New Delhi-110020, Phone : 011-51611861, Fax : 011-51611866
E-mail info@diamondpublication.com, Website: www.diamondpublication.com